Lerner and Loewe's
Gigi

Music by
FREDERICK LOEWE

Book & Lyrics by
ALAN JAY LERNER

Based on the novel by
Colette

Vocal Score

Piano Reduction by
TRUDE RITTMANN

Chappell & Co., Inc.

Synopsis of Scenes

Act I

Scene 1: A park, then a restaurant
in the Bois de Boulogne

Scene 2: Mamita's apartment
immediately following

Scene 3: Aunt Alicia's apartment
a short time later

Scene 4: a. Transition to the restaurant of the Eiffel Tower
b. Restaurant of the Eiffel Tower
evening

Scene 5: Stage L—Aunt Alicia's apartment
Stage R—Honoré's dressing room
early afternoon, the following day

Scene 6: Mamita's apartment
three weeks later, in late afternoon
a. En route to Trouville
immediately following

Scene 7: a. Lobby of the Grand Hotel, Trouville
b. The beach at Trouville
the following afternoon

Act II

Scene 1: Mamita's apartment
four weeks later, in mid-afternoon

Scene 2: The street outside Mamita's apartment
immediately following

Scene 3: Legal office of Mâitre Dufresne
a day or two later

Scene 4: Mamita's apartment
the following day

Scene 5: A street cafe
an hour later

Scene 6: Mamita's apartment
later that day

Scene 7: Maxim's
that night

Scene 8: Mamita's apartment
immediately following

Instrumentation

Flute/Piccolo, Oboe/Flute/B♭ Clarinet, B♭ Clarinet, B♭ Clarinet/Bass Clarinet/Flute, Bassoon; 2 Horns, 3 Trumpets, 2 Trombones; Percussion, Piano/Celesta, Harp; 6 Violin I, 4 Violin II, 2 Violas, 2 Violoncellos, Contrabass.

Gigi

First Performance, November 13, 1973
in the Uris Theatre, New York

The Los Angeles & San Francisco Civic Light Opera Production

Produced by EDWIN LESTER and SAINT-SUBBER

Directed by JOSEPH HARDY

Dances and Music Numbers Staged by Onna White

Scenic Production Designed by Oliver Smith
Costumes Designed by Oliver Messel
Lighting by Thomas Skelton

Musical Direction by Ross Reimueller
Orchestrations by Irwin Kostal
Dance Arrangements by Trude Rittmann
Musical Associate Harper MacKay
Associate Dance Director Martin Allen
Production Manager Bill Holland

Cast of Characters

Honoré Lachailles ....Alfred Drake
Gaston Lachailles ....Daniel Massey
Liane d'Exelmans ....Sandahl Bergman
Inez Alvarez (Mamita) ....Maria Karnilova
Gigi ....Karin Wolfe
Aunt Alicia ....Agnes Moorehead
Charles, her butler ....Gordon de Vol
Head Waiter, Receptionist, Telephone Installer,
    Maître d'Hotel ....Joe Ross
Two Waiters ....Leonard John Crofoot, Thomas Stanton
Liane's Dance Partner ....Thomas Anthony
An Artist ....Patrick Spohn
A Count ....Joel Pressman
Sandomir ....Randy di Grazio
Dancing Teacher ....Gregory Drotar
Manuel ....Truman Gaige
Maître du Fresne ....George Gaynes
Maître Duclos ....Howard Chitjian
Two Law Clerks ....Leonard John Crofoot, Thomas Stanton

The Ensemble: Thomas Anthony, Alvin Beam, Russ Beasley, Robyn
Blair, Leonard John Crofoot, Gordon de Vol, Randy di Grazio, John
Dorrin, Gregory Drotar, Janis Eckhart, Margit Haut, Andy Keyser,
Beverly Kopels, Diane Lauridsen, Merilee Magnuson, Kelley Max-
well, Vickie Patik, Joel Pressman, Patrick Spohn, Thomas Stanton,
Cherie Suzanne, Marie Tillmanns, Sallie True.

Little Girls: Patricia Daly, Jill Turnbull

Musical Program

ACT I

ACT II

GIGI
Overture

Grandioso (in 1)

Piano

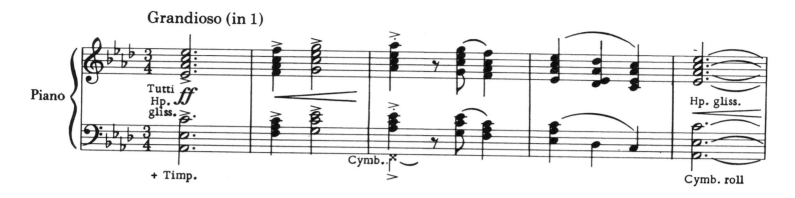

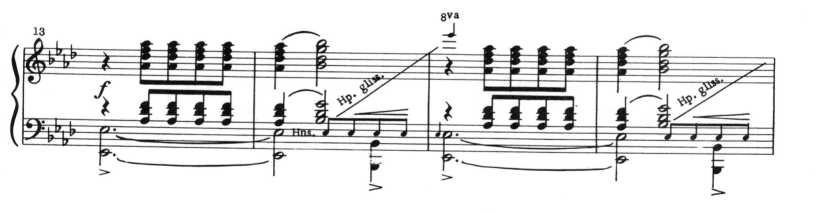

Honoré enters, addresses the audience:
Good Evening. . .
Bon Voyage. . .
Happy Birthday. . .

(He continues over music)
Good Evening because it is.

Allegretto grazioso

(Dialogue continues)

(Cue to continue)
Happy Birthday
because it's hers.

(Gigi blows
out candles)

(Gigi runs to birthday cake)
Presto (in 1)

Her name is Gigi. And she is
our raison d'être. The reason
we are here and you are there.

One. . .   Two. . .   Three. . .

(tremolo continues)

Now where shall we begin? *(Dialogue continues)*

Cue to continue:
Bois de Boulogne.

Scrim rises.
Lights come up on a crowded
Restaurant in the Bois de Boulogne.

Allegro (Polka)

Dialogue

No. 1   Thank Heaven For Little Girls

Cue: HONORÉ: . . . those who do not are usually women.

HONORÉ:

Now for ex - am - ple here we find   Ex - hib - it

A: the mar - ried kind.   These la - dies stood their

ground and won,   And I sa - lute them ev - 'ry one.

14

Here are some oth - ers to be - hold For whom the

bells have nev - er tolled. Oh, what a poor de -

heav - en _____ for lit - tle girls! _____ They

grow up in the most de - light - ful way. _____ Those

lit - tle eyes so help - less and ap - peal - ing _____ One day will

flash and send you crash - ing through the ceil - ing. _____ Thank

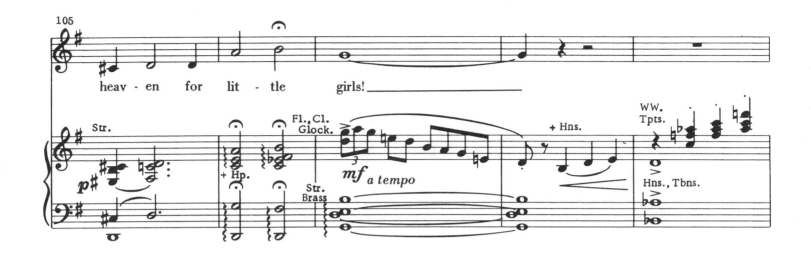

heav - en for lit - tle girls! _____

If this story is about a little girl, . . .*(dialogue continues)*

. . . what you have

No. 2

It's A Bore

Cue: HONORÉ: . . . You can't be bored at your age.

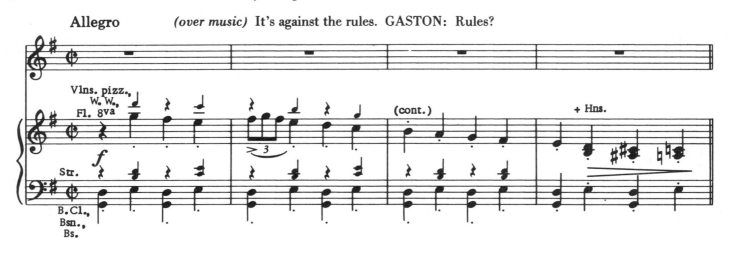

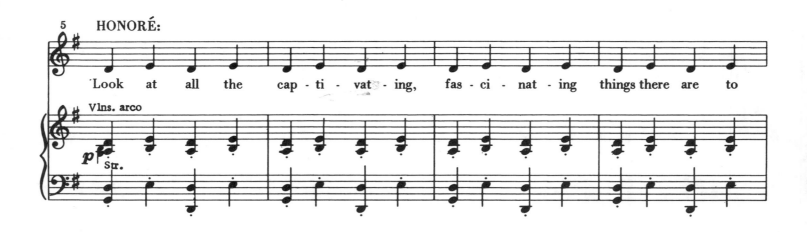

hear ev - 'ry tree al - most say - ing: Look at me! GASTON: What color are the trees?

HONORÉ: Green. GASTON: What color were they last year? HONORÉ: Green. GASTON: And next year? HONORÉ: Green. It's a

GASTON:

HONORÉ:

bore._____ Don't you mar - vel at the pow'r of the might - y Eif - fel

Tow'r, Know - ing there it will re - main ev - er - more?_____

Climb-ing up to the sky, O-ver nine-ty sto-ries high... GASTON:

How many stories? HONORÉ: Ninety. GASTON: How many yesterday? HONORÉ: Ninety. GASTON: And tomorrow?

HONORÉ: Ninety. GASTON: HONORÉ:

It's a bore._____ The riv-er Seine...!_____

GASTON: HONORÉ:

All it can do is flow._____ But think of wine!_____

28

No. 2A

It's A Bore - Incidental
(Change of Scene)

GASTON: I'm afraid I'm not as young as you are, Uncle. *(Dialogue continues)*

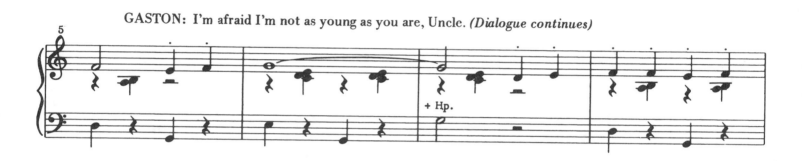

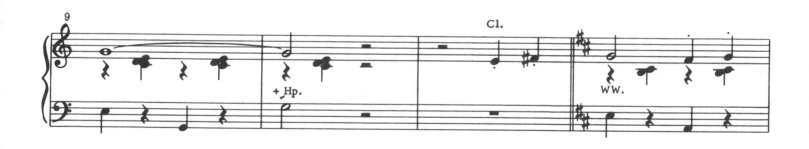

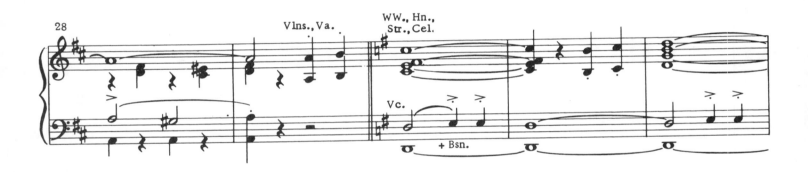

HONORÉ:
... then I suppose I did. Yes, I suppose I did.

(Gaston exits)

(Mamita enters)

Dialogue

No. 3   The Earth And Other Minor Things

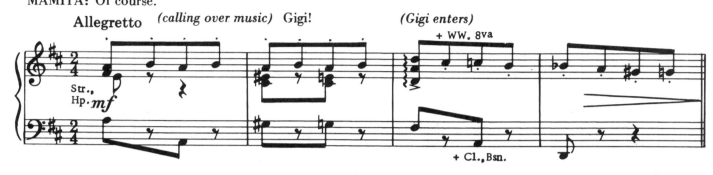

all it seems to be a ques-tion of; _____ A pau-per or a

slave or Aunt A-li-cia-- _____ But not a men-tion an-y-where of

love. _____ What is there that an-y-one can teach ____

____ If ev-'ry-thing I want is out of reach? _____ I

all?

I don't be-long where the crowds are.

I don't be-long where the clouds are. Then where do

I be long?

Segue

No. 3A

Change Of Scene

No. 4

Paris Is Paris Again

Cue: ALICIA: . . . Come along. It's dinner time.

Par - is is Par - is a - gain.

Lov - ers in clos - ets and shoes in the drawer,

Screams on the Rue Ma - de - leine;

Swords in the park! A shot in the dark! And

52

No. 5   She Is Not Thinking Of Me

Cue: GASTON: Anything. Anything.

So dis- arm - ing;___ Soft and charm - ing;___ She is not

think - ing of me!___ No, she's not think - ing of

me!___ In her eyes to - night___ There's a glow to - night___

They're so bright they could light Fon - taine - bleau to - night.___ She's so___

Is it that count with the mus-cles?

(The Strong Man)
Pomposo

Is it Jacques? Or Lé - on?

Oh, she's hot But it's not for Gas - ton!

No. 5A Change Of Scene

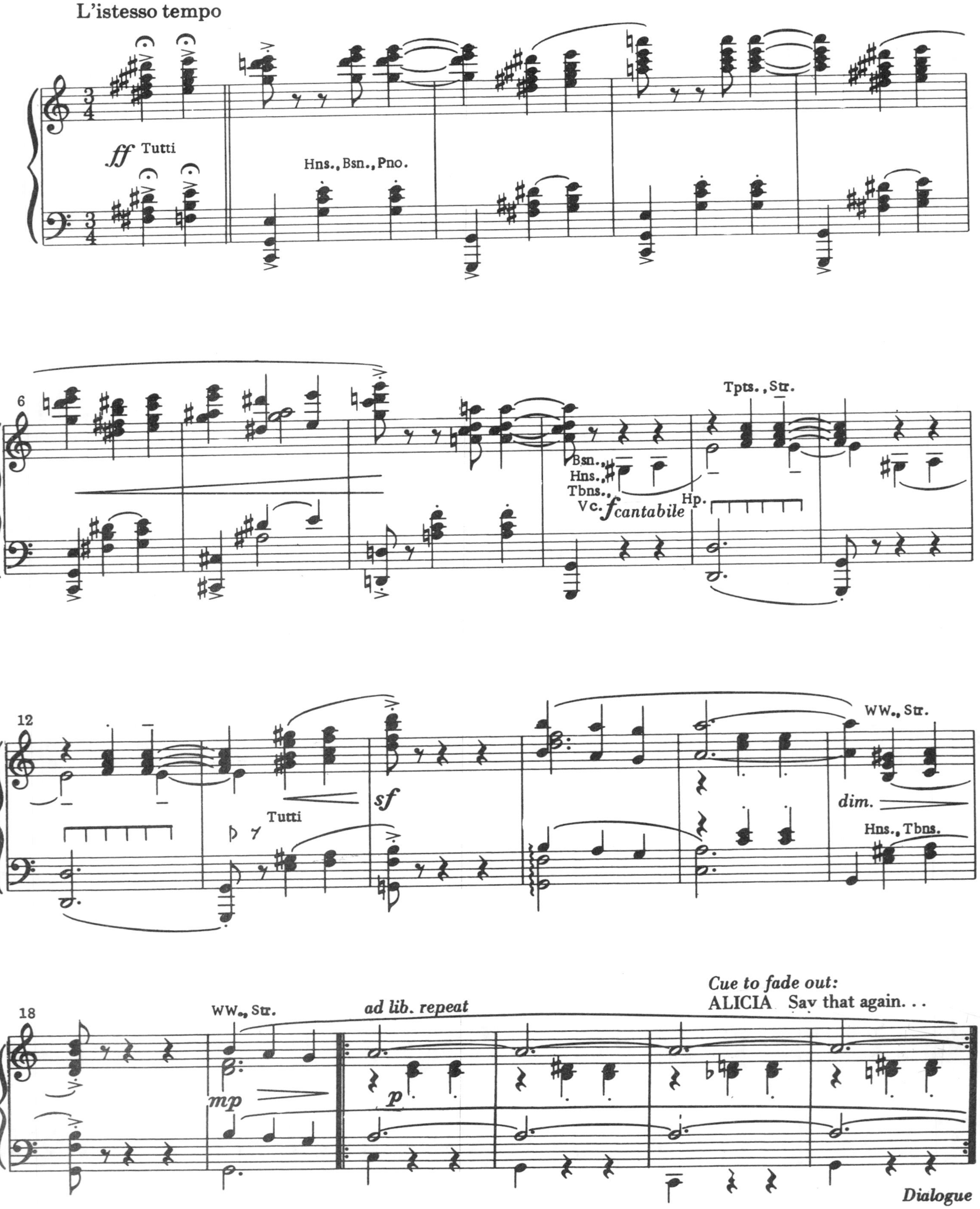

No. 6   It's A Bore (1st Reprise)

Cue: HONORÉ: A bore. Not at all.

No. 6A It's A Bore (2nd Reprise)

Cue: GASTON: Oh no! HONORÉ: Oh yes!

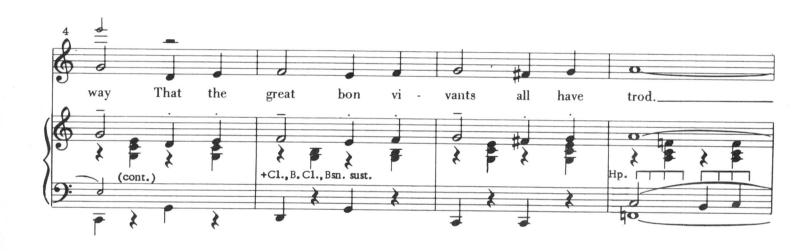

Till the dawn ev - 'ry day You must go the mer - ry

way That the great bon vi - vants all have trod._____

You must shine with a smile That would shame a croc - o - dile...

GASTON:
I must
do what?

No. 7 The Night They Invented Champagne

Cue: GASTON: It'll be marvelous fun.

ev - 'ry - one in sight_____ That since the world be -

gan No wom - an or a man Has ev - er been as

hap - py as we are_____ to

night!

GASTON:
The

No. 7A The Night They Invented Champagne

(Encore)

Cue: GIGI: The ocean!!

Dialogue

Part II

Cue: HONORÉ: Ah! Madame LaVerne...

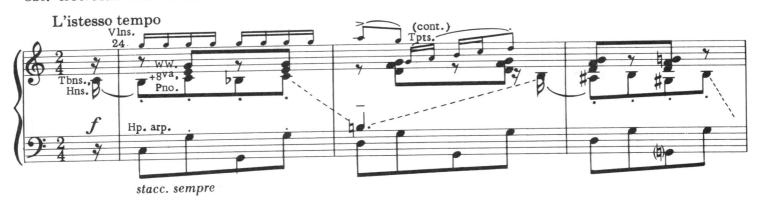

Dialogue

Part III

Cue: HONORÉ: Then who?

Part IV

Cue: ALICIA: Charles, take the luggage to the second floor. *(2nd time)*

No. 8   I Remember It Well

Cue: MAMITA: . . . the most endearing excuse for infidelity I have ever heard.

HONORÉ: *(music begins)* But I've never forgotten you. I remember that last night we were together as if it were yesterday.

* Also cued for WW.

No. 9   I Never Want To Go Home Again

FINALE - ACT I

GIGI: *a piacere*

If I had a wish, I would be a fish, e - ven just a clam.

Leave me here, I beg, here for - ev - er ex - act - ly where I am...

Allegro moderato (in 1)

Cue: GASTON:
Gigi!!

Cue to continue:
GASTON: Gigi, come here!   ALICIA: Inez. . . come here. . . *(dialogue continues)*

Meno mosso (in 1)

* Solo Vln. plays all tutti's, but senza sord., from here to end of Act I.

No. 10

Entr'acte

No. 11

Opening Act II
(The Telephone)

French, Ma - dame. It's French! What's wrong with you to - day?

Dialogue

No. 11A The New Dress

Cue: MAMITA: Oh, Gaston, you spoil her so.

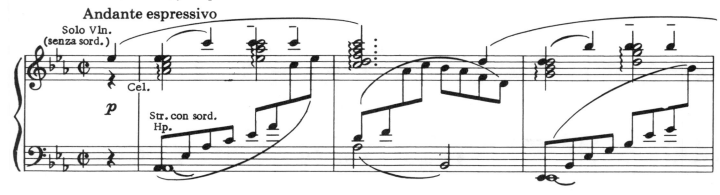

GIGI: Four yards of material in the skirt. Don't I look regal?

Dialogue

No. 12

Gigi

Cue: GASTON: Compromised indeed!

Allegro furioso

quipped and un-de-sir-a-ble to men.

(spoken) Of course, I

must in truth con-fess, That in that brand new lit - tle dress, She looked sur-

pris - ing-ly ma-ture And had a def - i - nite al - lure. It was a

shock, in fact, to me, A most a - maz-ing shock to see The way it clung On one so

148 grow-ing up be-fore my eyes._____ Gi - gi, you're not at

152 all that fun - ny, awk - ward lit - tle girl I knew! Oh,

155 no! O - ver night there's been a breath - less change in

158 you. Oh, Gi - gi, while you were trem-bling on the brink Was I out

191 Gi - gi, while you were trem - bling on the brink. Was I out

193 yon - der some - where blink - ing at a star? Oh, Gi - gi, have I been

196 Più mosso
stand - ing up too close or back too far?_____ When did your

199 spar - kle turn to fi - re? And your warmth be - come de - si - re? Oh, what

203

mir - a - cle has made you the way you are?

allargando

Hns.

+ Timp. roll

Tpts.

ff Hns., Tbns.

+ Timp.

Segue

No. 12A   Gigi - End of Scene

Maestoso

Str., WW. 8va, Hns., Tpts.

Tutti ff *molto marcato*

Bsn., Vc., C Bs.

Timp. Tbns., Pno.

GASTON: Mamita, do you have a lawyer... I have a
business matter to discuss with you...
A very serious business matter...

poco allargando

Cymb.

Hp. gliss.

+ Timp. roll

Timp.

*Attacca No. 13
as one*

The Contract

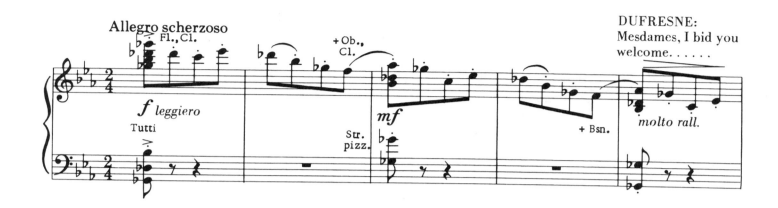

Andante, molto rubato

dame, I have been de-sig-nat-ed by Gas-ton Al-
bert Phi-lippe La-chailles To no-ti-fy you of his pas-sion for your
niece. And fur-ther, With-out her per-ma-nent com-pan-ion-ship My
cli-ent feels his hap-pi-ness will cease. So in the cus-tom-ar-y gen-tle-man-ly

205

DUFRESNE:

rooms! _____ Dear, oh dear, what is wrong with this pen? _____

210 **ALICIA:**

_____ Sev - en rooms! _____ Sev - en rooms! _____ All to -

215 **ALL:**

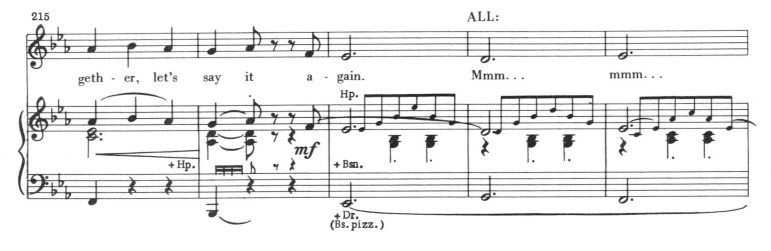

geth - er, let's say it a - gain. Mmm. . . mmm. . .

220

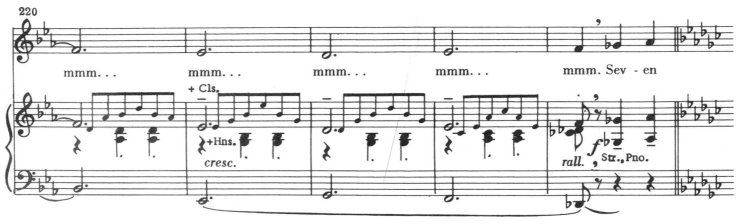

mmm. . . mmm. . . mmm. . . mmm. . . mmm. Sev - en

433

la _____ Tra - la - la. _____ Lit - tle Gi - gi is

438 Deciso (in 3)

fi - n'lly in love. Gi - gi is fi - n'lly Se - cure - ly, di - vine - ly in

WW., Hns., Str., Pno.

allargando

444 Piu mosso (in 1)

love! _____ love! _____

WW., Str., Pno. Tpts.

Hns.

f Tbn.

+ Tbn.

Hns., Tbn.

+ Tbns.

Cymb. x

451 Presto

love! _____

WW., Str.

Bsn., Hns., Brass, Pno.

Vc.

(cont.)

ff (Hp. gliss.) *sf*

Timp. roll (cont.)

Segue

Change of Scene 3

* In the Broadway production, the first ending was omitted.

No. 13B   Change of Scene 4

Cue: Mamita throws a cushion at the bedroom door.

Allegro furioso

Cue to fade:
GASTON: Uncle...
HONORE: Gaston...

Repeat ad lib.

Dialogue

No. 14   I'm Glad I'm Not Young Anymore

Cue: HONORE: Adieu, my boy.

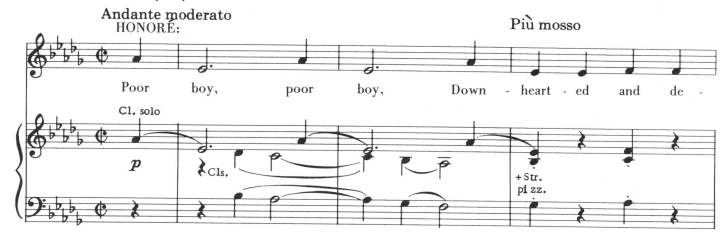

fu - sion, No morn-ing - af-ter sur-prise;_____ No self-de-

lu - sion_____ That when you're tell-ing those lies, she is-n't wise. And

e - ven if love comes through the door, The kind that goes on for-ev-er-more, For-

ev-er-more is short-er than be-fore.____ Oh, I'm so

A tempo (Poco marcato)

45

glad — that I'm — not young an — y —

49

more. — The ti — ny re — mark that

52

tor — tures you, The fear that your friends won't like her too; I'm

55

glad I'm not young an — y — more. — The

No. 14A   I'm Glad I'm Not Young Anymore

Encore

Lostesso tempo

HONORE:

The wor-ry if you're the best or worst, And

then you find out that you're the first.

All oth-ers but you she may en-chant. You

170

not for a week-end hon-ey-moon; What bet-ter life could heav-en have in store?

Oh, I'm so glad ___ that I'm ___ not young

an - y - more! ___

No. 14B Change of Scene

(Hold until lights up for next scene)

Dialogue

No. 15   In This Wide, Wide World

Cue: MAMITA: Gigi?!... Who is this?   *(Gigi takes the telephone receiver from Mamita)*

GIGI: Gaston?

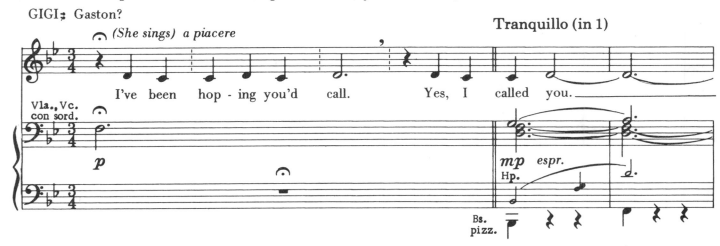

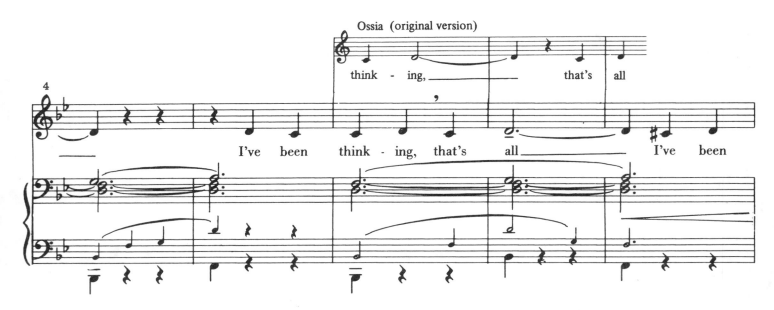

44
lore, she'll have; Much more, she'll have, than I pos-sess; _____ With so much

46
A tempo
more fi-nesse _ and style; _____ Some-one used to this wide, _____ wide

49
world _____ Who can love _ and still not hope too high: _____ Who can

52
live your life And give your life The things I can't sup-ply! And if you

Segue

End of Scene

ALICIA: That sweet child!
I never lost faith
in her.

Segue as one

No. 16

At Maxim's
(Can-Can)

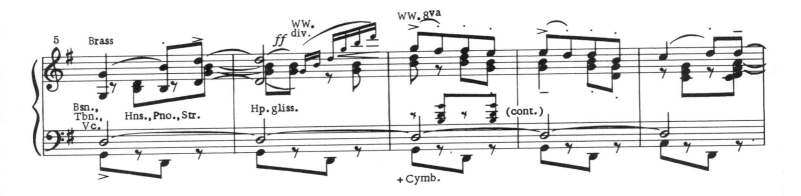

Presto (Can-can)

Dialogue

No. 16A

Waltz Underscore
(At Maxim's)

Cue: GIGI: Dipped.
    GASTON: Dipped?
    GIGI: Dipped.

Tempo di Valse, moderato

GIGI: What's in your breast pocket? *(Dialogue continues)*

To 2nd ending on cue:
GASTON: Wouldn't you like
the lady in the powder room
to help you?

Repeat ad lib.

(Dialogue continues)

Cue to Attacca No. 16B:
HONORE: What?
GIGI: Gaston!!

Repeat ad lib.

Attacca

No. 16B   Can-Can and Change of Scene

Cue: GIGI: Gaston!!

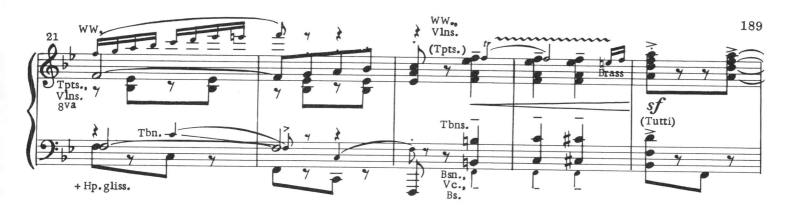

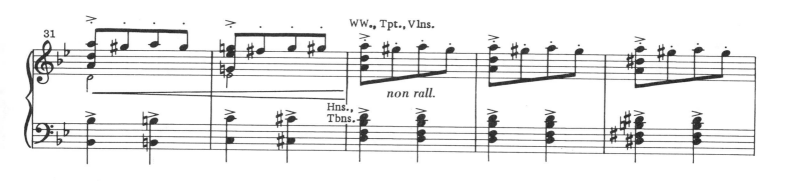

Maestoso *(Gaston enters)*

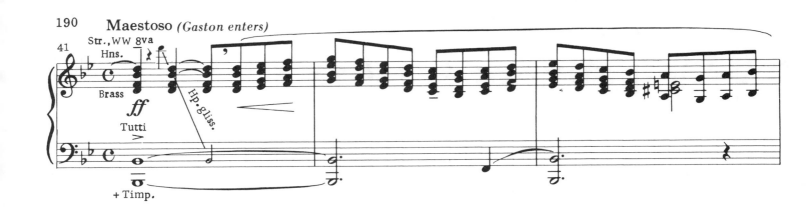

(Hold till lights up on next scene)

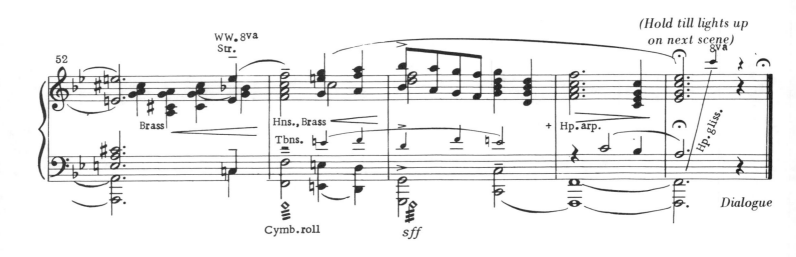

Dialogue

No. 17 Thank Heaven for Little Girls

Reprise - Finale Act II

Cue: MAMITA: Thank heaven. . .
HONORE: . . . for little girls. . .

Thank heav-en for them all No mat-ter where, no mat-ter who With-out them what would lit-tle boys do? Thank heav-en. . . Thank heav-en. . . Thank heav-en for lit-tle girls!

No. 18

Curtain Calls

Segue

No. 19

Exit Music

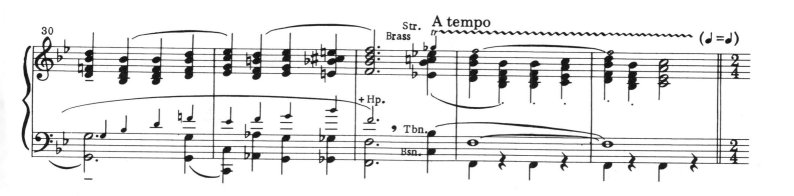